D1218896

BRITAIN IN PICTURES
THE BRITISH PEOPLE IN PICTURES

ENGLISH GARDENS

GENERAL EDITOR
W. J. TURNER

The Editor is most grateful to all those who have
so kindly helped in the selection of illustrations
especially to officials of the various public
Museums Libraries and Galleries and
to all others who have generously
allowed pictures and MSS
to be reproduced

ENGLISH GARDENS

HARRY ROBERTS

WITH
8 PLATES IN COLOUR
AND
23 ILLUSTRATIONS IN
BLACK & WHITE

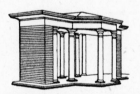

COLLINS · 14 ST. JAMES'S PLACE · LONDON
MCMXLVII

PRODUCED BY
ADPRINT LIMITED LONDON

FIRST PUBLISHED 1944
THIRD IMPRESSION 1947

PRINTED IN GREAT BRITAIN BY
CLARKE & SHERWELL LTD NORTHAMPTON
ON MELLOTEX BOOK PAPER MADE BY
TULLIS RUSSELL & CO LTD MARKINCH SCOTLAND

LIST OF ILLUSTRATIONS

BLACK AND WHITE ILLUSTRATIONS

ANNUALS
Coloured engraving from
C. McIntosh's *Flower Garden*, 1838

INTRODUCTION

A PERSONAL NOTE

GARDENERS, and the owners of gardens, are of many kinds. Until comparatively recent times, the English cottager—as well as the English farmer and village parson—though resentful of further intrusions on what long usage had taught him were his natural rights—has nearly always looked on the great landowner, the local squire, and all his possessions, with admiration and respect. Thus it is that, from the days of our early history up to the last half-century or so, by the English Garden has been generally understood the large garden of the well-to-do. The owners of many of these are themselves practical and keen garden-lovers, though they may employ half-a-dozen professionals to do the major part of the physical work involved. But, more often than not, the squire has been quite ignorant of and uninterested in gardening—

7

looking upon his garden merely as a means of impressing his humbler neighbours and, if possible, of provoking the envy of rival garden-owners. There has thus been afforded great opportunity for active competition between professional head-gardeners ; and it is, in fact, chiefly to them and to a few eccentric employers that the fashions in gardening with which this book is so largely concerned have hitherto been due.

Actually, gardeners of a more modest kind display great differences in the considerations by which they are motivated. Some are simple utilitarians, many being concerned only with the need of growing the maximum of food for their families. Others, less economically hampered, look on the garden not as a means of directly satisfying any sense of beauty, but as an instrument whereby another aesthetic sense—that of flavour and delicacy in fruit and vegetables—may be gratified. Then, again, there are people who use their ground as a sort of botanic garden, their interest in that science being stronger than their sense of architectural fitness. Travellers and explorers have brought back from abroad all sorts of shrubs, orchids, and other plants ; while intrepid collectors and agents of enterprising commercial firms have searched remote parts of South America, Africa, China, Japan and other countries for new beauties wherewith to enrich English gardens. Many gardeners again, are influenced mainly by memories of some garden with, for them, happy associations; while yet others are plant-lovers rather than garden-lovers. Poetic and literary associations also play their part. To some extent this explains the centuries-old conflict between the apostles of garden formalism and those of so-called landscapism. The alternate reaction from one to the other through the centuries has been due to the tendency of the more fanatic disciples of each school to carry its dogmas to ridiculous extremes.

In the present century Britain has been engaged in two great wars, conducted on novel lines, with novel weapons ; the total effect of which

DELPHINIUM GRANDIFLORUM
Coloured engraving after Roscoe
From Havell's *Floral Illustrations*, 1831

on gardening in this country is bound to be immense. Already one sees a great reduction in the number of large gardens in private hands. The cultivation of flowers except on the smallest scale is discouraged, and large estates all over the country are being split up for building development. After the war, nearly all gardens in private hands will be essentially villa gardens or cottage gardens. We shall then see who among us are real gardeners. It is a commonplace of art that beauty and fitness are almost synonyms; and it may be doubted if any garden in which the individuality and true character of the plants grown are not respected and given full scope for expression can ever give rise to that emotion which true beauty evokes. Yet there must be a certain amount of deliberate planning. There must be paths, and we shall find by observation that some arrangements of these paths and of the plants please us more than others. The smaller the garden, in many ways the more import-

GREAT DAFFODIL
Engraving from *The Complete Florist*, 1740

ant its planning. For every false note will here assert itself ; and, where every yard is within eyesight, distance, affectation and deliberate complexity will be seen for what they are. But never mistake the planning of the garden for its end. Just as the best and most skilfully planned house would be less than nothing were it not adapted to foster healthy and happy human lives, so a garden, whatever may be the architectural skill shown in its designing, will yet be sterile and functionless if it fails to provide a congenial home for the plants which are its true inhabitants. "Of so many sweet floures to chuse the best, it is hard, seeing they be all so good." So speaks the true flower-lover and garden-lover. The greatest joy which a garden can yield is a feeling of restfulness and peace, a feeling which no garden of staring beds and ostentatious

9

splendour can afford, but which is yielded—as by nothing else in the world—by an old-fashioned garden of happy, homely, old-fashioned flowers. By an old-fashioned garden I mean an informal "garden of all sorts of pleasant flowers which our English ayre will permitt to be noursed up," as Parkinson put it ; and by old-fashioned flowers I mean Sweet Williams, Carnations or Gilly-flowers, Mignonette, Sweet Peas, Roses and Honeysuckles, "Daffodils, Fritillarias, Iacinthes, Saffron-flowers, Lillies, Flowerdeluces, Tulipas, Anemones, French Cowslips, or Beares eares and such other flowers, very beautifull, delightfull and pleasant." After the severe, monotonous, formal arrangements which still too often constitute the gardens around some of our finest houses, how interesting and restful it is to stroll round some delightful old garden, where the shape of the beds and borders is not prearranged, where all the soil is occupied, where every plant looks healthy and at home, where every yard brings one a surprise and a fresh interest, where the old walls have growing from their crevices such plants as the Cheddar Pink, Sedums and Sempervivums; where, too, every plant in its glory hides the decay of its predecessor in bloom and shelters the birth of its successor.

It is because I have always had much in common with the gardening cottager that I here venture on a small bit of personal history. This may help the reader to understand what may seem at times an undue bias in my narration of the strictly historical ups and downs of English gardening, for or against some piece of formalism or landscapism.

Most of the "moulding" hours of the first ten years of my life were spent in a roomy, detached house with a large orchard and two spacious high-walled gardens on the lower slopes of the Quantock Hills, a few hundred feet above the fertile valley known as Taunton Vale. At a very early age, I went as a day scholar to a small preparatory school in the village. My school hours made little impression on my "interest." All my real life, from my fifth or sixth birthday, was spent in my home, the gardens and orchard attached thereto, and the meadows of neighbouring farms.

I used to enjoy co-operating with my mother, who had charge of our flower-garden ; accompanying her on occasional excursions to fields where she collected in a basket certain special soils for the culture of fastidious flowers. When I was less than seven years old, I was allotted a small strip of border under a sandstone wall, for my very own, to grow what I liked in. Someone had given me a little book called *Gardening for Children*, with coloured plates of flowers ; of a number of these I begged cuttings or seeds from my mother and from neighbours. Later, I came across some little books on the natural history of butterflies, beetles and wild flowers. I soon became interested in all these things, and used to hunt for them in the lanes and ditches. I became a "collector," and asked my parents if I might have a small, unused room for my "museum."

THE BLAND AMARYLLIS
Coloured engraving from *Paxton's Flower Garden*, 1851-52

I grew more and more interested in the habits of these plants and animals, and was inclined to look at garden plants from the point of view of their likings and "natural" ways of life ; getting early to the stage at which that celebrated gardener, Canon Ellacombe, eventually arrived ; so that if I found that a plant had spread from its position in the border to the middle of the gravel path, where it was obviously more at home, I preferred rather to change the path, than to disturb the plant. I can truly say that my precocious interest in science and my increasing susceptibility to every sort of human and literary association have left me with a really catholic taste in gardens and in gardening.

More than forty-five years ago, I contributed a series of articles to *The Gardener's Chronicle*. The fact that Dr. Masters, the critical editor of that admirable paper, *The Times of Horticulture*, as it has been called, considered these articles worthy of a place in his columns, induced me to assemble them in book form, under the title, *The Chronicle of a Cornish Garden*. I sent my manuscript to Mr. John Lane of the Bodley Head, and although it was unlike any books he had previously published—for the Bodley Head was, of course, associated with such books as the Keynotes Series and The Yellow Book, and such artists as Aubrey Beardsley —he decided to bring out my little book, which was, I think, the first volume to be illustrated by that distinguished artist, F. L. B. Griggs. It has been out of print for thirty years or more. In my opening chapter I made it clear that my garden was really a very modest affair, no realisation of the Baconian ideal, but a small piece of ground enclosed by low walls on all sides, and, when I took possession of it, a more hopeless, irregular, poverty-struck patch, covered as it was with bindweed, couch-grass and other weeds, it would tax the utmost patience to discover.

My predecessor took no interest in gardening, and considered the possibilities of the situation not such as to merit much expenditure of time or money. And truly it did look a hopeless task to extract much beauty from it. But I thought of Virgil's contented old Corycian, who acquired possession of a few acres of waste land which was not worth ploughing, of no value for pasturage, and quite useless for vine-growing ; yet by steady perseverance and hopefulness this genuine old gardener made things grow everywhere, and was enabled to cover his supper-table with dainties of his own growing. He was always able to pick the earliest rose in spring and the first autumn fruit ; and even when winter cracked the ground with frosts, he still had flowers in sheltered nooks with which to cheer himself and nourish his bees.

Unfortunately, I had not even come into a few acres of neglected land, but I saw that, if I were to maintain my interest in gardening and show myself to be a worthy descendant of the veteran of the Georgics, I must make the best of what I had until such time as Fate should give me the garden which my mind had ever imaged. So I fortified myself with recollections of pioneers faced with difficulties even greater than mine. Gardening readers will remember Dean Hole's story of the enthusiastic flower-loving navvy who, obtaining the post of gate-keeper on the railway, was provided with nothing but a barren gravel-pit as apology for a garden. "Twelve months afterwards," says the Dean, "I came near the place again —was it a mirage I saw on the sandy desert ? There were vegetables, fruit-bushes and fruit-trees, all in vigorous health ; there were flowers, and the flower-queen in all her beauty. 'Why, Will,' I exclaimed, 'what have you done to the gravel-bed ?' 'Lor bless yer,' he replied, grinning, 'I hadn't been here a fortnight afore I swopped it for a pond !' He had, as a further explanation informed me, and after agreement with a neigh-bouring farmer, removed with pick and barrow his sandy stratum to the depth of three feet, wheeled it to the banks of an old pond, or rather to the margin of a cavity where a pond once was, but which had been gradually filled up with leaves and silt ; and this rich productive mould he had brought home a distance of two hundred yards, replacing it with the gravel, and levelling as per contract."

PICKING HONEYSUCKLE
Water colour by H. D. Copsey

To return to my little garden. First of all, I thoroughly broke up the ground, cleaned it of all weeds as far as possible, and incorporated a heavy dressing of manure. I saw that it was useless to hope that the weeds were conquered, so I decided to grow nothing for a season but vegetable crops, which would necessitate the ground being dug and cleaned a few more times. I took time by the forelock, however, and planted a number of pyramidal fruit-trees in the autumn. Continual forking, digging, manuring and weeding made the soil such as will produce fruit and flowers. Paths were made, and borders naturally were produced ; seeds were sown, and bulbs planted ; a small greenhouse and frame were built, and the little plot began to look like an adjunct to a human dwelling. As the garden was entirely overlooked by every passing train—the railway arching over the valley on whose slope my garden lay—I planted standard fruit and other trees to cut off that view as far as may be. You see, I am English and like to ply my hobby in privacy. For I hold that a garden is a place whither one should be able to retire from the *profanum vulgus*—like a

13

private study, like even silence itself, in that we may thence defy the outside world. This is an aim which the true gardener should bear ever in mind. The grandeur and glory of the forest, the hill and the plain are quite other than anything which the garden can give. This is as certain as the truth that no library can serve as a real substitute for the world of men.

The profound emotion that we term melancholy, which grand scenery induces, is usually absent from the garden effect. Gardening, on the other hand, is calculated to breed in its devotees a feeling of quiet content-ment, mainly—we may suppose—because it is constantly telling the gardener of his power in obtaining desired and beautiful results. Fully as much as angling, gardening is truly "the contemplative man's recreation." Raising giant flowers for competition at flower-shows is scarcely the sort of thing I mean. The gardening which attracts me is on a footing with old Izaak Walton's fishing. I like to be my own gardener, and I take an interest in my plants as individual living things, as well as bits of beautiful colour and form. I like to see a plant grow and develop, to study its distinctive features and their causes, and to read about it and so learn what others have observed. A small, convenient and healthy house, a large and well-situated garden, a good library gradually accumulated, a small competency—and what more in the way of physical possessions can the contemplative man require ?

The Englishman's love of gardens and of gardening is one of the most characteristic things about him. Beautiful flowers provoke enthusiasm in the one-room tenements of Stepney and in the Mayfair drawing-room alike. It is, indeed, pathetic to witness the persistence of this beautiful trait—the love of gardens—in the most unpromising slums of our cities. Worlidge, writing in 1680, says that "there is scarcely a cottage in most of the southern parts of England but hath its proportionable garden ; so great delight do most men take in it." And that it still flourishes, at any rate in the southern half of England, is shown by the following short passage, taken from a London daily newspaper published in early February, 1943 :

"While the official date of its arrival is still forty-five days distant, Spring has indeed been in the air since November. People in this office with gardens have some quite impressive evidence of it. M.R., military reporter, has polyanthuses, primulas, gilly-flowers—even roses—in bloom. G.H., features editor, says that there are two crocuses in her garden. F.L., sub-editor, was gathering primroses in his Dorset garden a month ago. There are snowdrops and crocuses there now as well. W.H. says aconites in his garden began to bloom earlier than usual, while daffodils have a six-inch growth of leaf."

It is impossible for the most *blasé* townsman to walk through one of those beautiful villages distributed throughout the south-west of England

THE PRIORY GARDEN, THE PRIORY, WOLLASTON
Wash drawing by Michael Rothenstein, 1940

without being moved by the little gardens that front the cottages on either side of the road. What is it that is so moving? We are not moved in this way by the flower-beds round the Albert Memorial. Yet there can be no doubt that the latter represent an altogether more definite conscious artistic purpose. Does not one of the great differences lie in this: that in the cottage garden the individuality and character and peculiar beauty of each plant is respected; whereas in the more formal and "artistic" garden the colours and forms of the individual plants are considered as almost nothing in themselves, but only as contributing to some striking mass effect? The typical amateur gardener in this country grows to love his plants almost in the same way as that in which a man is said to love his dog.

One of the greatest gifts of a perfect garden is the gift of solitude, and that is generally beyond the power of the little cottage plot to offer; but, as a source of infinite pleasure to its owner, as a source of pleasure to all who pass by, as a cheering feature of English landscape, and as a great force tending towards contentment and peace, the cottage garden is beyond all praise.

To return to my career as a garden writer. So pleased was John Lane with the reception given to the *Chronicle of a Cornish Garden*, that he asked me to edit a series of Handbooks of Practical Gardening. At the end of the *Chronicle*, I had given a few supplemental hints for those who shared my ideas ; among them a selection of tall and dwarf border plants—including, of course, herbaceous plants—hints on constructing a small rock garden, a list of winter-blooming plants, and a list of works on gardening that I had found interesting, suggestive and helpful. This list included first of all Robinson's *English Flower Garden*, his *Hardy Flowers*, and *Wild Garden*, Ellacombe's *In a Gloucestershire Garden*, Bright's *Year in a Lancashire Garden*, Watson's *Flowers and Gardens*, Jekyll's *Wood and Garden*, and Amherst's *History of Gardening in England*. I should have added Parkinson's *Paradisus* and Kerner and Oliver's *Natural History of Plants*.

These books made up, and still do, my gardening Bible. Evidently I took Robinson's ideas as having settled the ancient controversy between the formalist school and their equally dogmatic opponents. Both Robinson and Miss Jekyll seemed to me, and still seem to me, to have intelligently settled the matter of garden construction for all real garden lovers and real plant lovers.

I wrote an early volume of the Handbooks myself. It was called *The Book of Old-Fashioned Flowers*, and was so relatively popular that a second edition had to be brought out a couple of years later. In that book, I give as my aim the teaching to those who are comparatively new to gardening the general principles which they must observe if they wish to grow successfully those flowering plants which are able to live their whole lives in the open air of this country. By old-fashioned flowers are meant those which we may class with the herbaceous, bulbous and other hardy plants which one always expects to find in the old cottage gardens, vicarage gardens and old farmhouse gardens of romance, and does occasionally find in those of reality.

One is continually discovering fresh old-fashioned people, and in like manner we are continually having additions made to our list of old-fashioned flowers. Many newly discovered or newly introduced plants therefore, were treated of in this book. Still, as a matter of fact, most of the flowers named in its pages are old favourites, and have long been grown and sentimentalised over by English gardeners and poets. No attempt was made to render the book a complete handbook of hardy flowers ; in the first place, the space at disposal would barely have served to enumerate them, and, in the second place, the thing had been done, and done admirably, by that great gardening writer, William Robinson, whose *English Flower Garden*, already referred to, is in many ways the most important work on gardening which has appeared since the time of Parkinson.

ROSES

Coloured engraving by Earlom after R. J. Thornton

From Thornton's *Temple of Flora or Garden of Nature*, 1799

DESIGN FOR A FLOWER GARDEN
From H. Repton's *Observations on the Theory and Practice of Landscape Gardening,* 1803

The flowers dealt with in my *Old-fashioned Flowers* are but a few of those worth growing, for nearly every plant, when allowed to develop freely and naturally, is full of interest and full of beauty. Everyone should decide for himself what he will grow in the particular environment he may have to offer. I have no faith in "laws" as to the arrangement of flowers with a view to producing "colour schemes," for I have never seen colour schemes which surpass those chance effects of the hedgerow or the meadow, or of those pleasant gardens where the gardener's sole aim is to grow plants from the plants' point of view—that is to say, with the sole aim of growing them healthily and well. Of course, occasionally, a bad colour shows itself, but the remedy is simple and obvious. Occasionally, too, a colour discord will be perceived in bed or border, but a spade will cure the trouble in five minutes. Indeed, there is some small risk at the present moment that the individuality of beautiful plants and flowers may be too frequently sacrificed to the production of "effects."

It will be generally agreed that an ideal garden should be so enclosed (*hortus*, an enclosed space) as to afford not only shelter to plants from the more strenuous forces of Nature, but also that privacy from the vulgar gaze which we call seclusion. If the garden is to be enclosed by walls, let these be of a fair height—not less than seven feet—and let them be clothed with a variety of the lovely climbing plants now at the disposal of the gardener. Although the evening is the best time for enjoying the flowers of our gardens during the months of July and August, few gardeners ever think of devoting any part of their gardens to flowers that bloom at night. Yet the pleasure to be obtained from them is very great, and the possible variety is considerable. Nearly all are fragrant, as otherwise it would be difficult in the darkness for them to attract the moths which they mostly require as pollen-bearers. The night gardener has a considerable field in which to work ; whilst to those who share Baudelaire's love of scents, the realm of night-blooming flowers should be a very Paradise.

> "Il est des parfums frais comme des chairs d'enfants,
> Doux comme les hautbois, verts comme les prairies,
> —Et d'autres, corrompus, riches et triomphants,
> Ayant l'expansion des choses infinies,
> Comme l'ambre, le musc, le benjoin et l'encens,
> Qui chantent les transports de l'esprit et des sens."

I have said that the beauty of a successful garden is due largely to the feeling of repose and settled-downness which it yields. Every plant should look, I feel, as though it "belongs" where it is, as though it always has been there, and as though there is no intention of shifting it in a week or two to some glass-house, store-room, or other site. The plants in many gardens look as though they have merely come to pay an afternoon call,

17

GARDEN AT CAMBRIDGE COTTAGE, KEW
Drawing by H. Walter

dressed exactly *à la mode*, speaking always "cumeelfo"—like the people of Troy Town, and elsewhere—giving one the certain knowledge that they will only say the right thing, look the right thing, and leave at the right time, unregretted and unmissed. The "comfortably-at-home" effect may be contributed to, largely, by three factors ; firstly the presence of abundant deciduous trees and shrubs, giving infinitely varied effects of light and shade ; secondly, the arrangement of the plants in bold groups of single species ; and, thirdly, the provision of each separate plant with depth of suitable soil and space to develop its individual form.

There is one book, difficult now to obtain, which contains a record of the truest and most careful study of flowers and of their beauty, which we have in the language. That book is called *Flowers and Gardens* by Dr. Forbes-Watson, and the following passage from its pages beautifully explains the sentiment of the gardener who grows mainly old-fashioned flowers, or, at any rate, flowers with which he has long been familiar:

"We make the acquaintance of any individual existence under an immense number of aspects, and it is the sum of all these aspects which constitutes that existence to us. A Snowdrop, for instance, is not to me merely such a figure as a painter might give me by copying the flower when placed so that its loveliness shall be best apparent, but a curious mental combination or selection from the figures which the flower may present when placed in every possible position and in every aspect which it has worn from birth to grave, and coloured by all the associations which have chanced to cling around it. To the bodily eye which beholds it for the first time, it might be of no consequence what lay within the petals, though even then the imagination might be whispering some solution of the secret; but to the eye of mind, when the flower has been often seen, that hidden green and yellow which is necessary to complete the harmony becomes distinctly visible—visible, that is, in that strange, indefinite way in which all things, however incompatible, seem present and blended together when the imaginative faculty is at work . . . We find the same principle at work in the feeling which compelled the old sculptors to finish the hidden side of the statue. They said, 'For the Gods are everywhere.' So it is with a really beautiful plant, and for this reason they who would obtain all the possible pleasure and beauty from their gardens should become, not gardeners only, but also botanists and students of poetry and of beautiful form."

AQUATIC PLANTS
Coloured engraving from
C. McIntosh's *Flower Garden*, 1838

W E have practically no records of life in Britain before its invasion by the Romans in B.C. 55 ; and, even then, we have only the not too reliable record of Julius Caesar. It is pretty certain, however, that nothing that could be called gardening was attempted, even if an occasional eccentric planted round his dwelling some wild strawberry plant or other wild edible fruit or vegetable he came across in his huntings. But the Roman occupation, which lasted some four or five hundred years, certainly brought and left behind it knowledge of gardens and their utilitarian, if not their aesthetic possibilities ; for in Rome itself, we know that gardens and the art of gardening had attained a fairly high degree of development ; and this not only among the richer classes but also among no inappreciable part of the better-to-do plebeians. In his *Natural History*, written in the first century A.D., Pliny the Elder tells us (in the words of his translator) that "And even in these our daies, under the name of Gardens and Hortyards, there goe many daintie places of pleasure within the very citie ; and under the colour also and title of them men are possessed of faire closes and pleasant fields, yea, and of proper houses with a good circuit of ground lying to them, like pretie fermes and graunges in the countrey ; all of which they tearme by the name of Gardens.

"And as for the other quarters set out with beds of floures and sweet smelling hearbs, what reckoning was made of them in old time may appear by this, that a man could not heretofore come by a commoner's house within the citie, but he could see the windowes beautified with green quishins [cushions] wrought and tapissed with floures of all colours ; resembling daily to their view the Gardens indeed which were in our villages, as being in the very heart of the citie, they might think themselves in the countrey. . ."

Considering the long period of the Roman occupation of Britain, and the elaboration of some of the architectural and other features of many of the Roman houses which archaeological research has revealed in this country, we can be pretty sure that gardens and gardening, though perhaps on a more modest scale than in Rome itself, were cultivated by the richer Latin settlers and officials during their stay here. The survival of the Latin names of so many fruits, herbs, and flowers confirms this supposition. Whether or no this was so, it is quite certain that gardening had no place here after the Roman Empire fell and Britain was again subjected to repeated invasions by various Continental barbarians. The Saxons were little more civilised than the other non-Latin Europeans who preceded them ; and gardening had again to wait for another civilising influence to operate here. That influence was furnished by the spread of Christianity and the establishment of monasteries ; among the monks being many

MARCH : PRUNING TREES
Illumination from *Queen Mary Psalter*, English MS. c. 1325

men of learning, who appreciated the pleasure and utility, spiritual as well as material, of such unwarlike arts and crafts as those of horticulture and the writing and reading of books. On the products of their gardens the monks depended for the materials of a large part of their routine dietaries, whilst their medical remedies mainly consisted of herbs which they themselves grew. Others they no doubt imported in a dry state from Continental monasteries, furnished with more congenial climates. In the twelfth century, it is recorded that Brithnodus, the first Abbot of Ely, improved the Abbey by constructing gardens and orchards around it : in these arts, he is reputed to have been highly skilled. And, in the same century, an orchard, vineyard and herbarium form part of the surroundings of the monastery at Canterbury. Of this we have pictorial evidence in the Great Psalter of Eadwin, now in the Library of Trinity College, Cambridge. Alexander Necham, who was born in 1157 and was made Director of the school attached to Dunstable Abbey whilst still in his twenties, in his *De Naturis Rerum*, gives an account of what he says a fine garden should consist and what plants it should contain. It is generally thought that this is mainly a list of plants which he grew in his garden at Cirencester (where, having joined the Augustines, he became Abbot in 1213).

In the eleventh and twelfth centuries, we find the times so troublous that small attempt at gardening—even the planting of vineyards—was made, apart from the monasteries. A few important houses were surrounded by pleasure grounds, with trimmed hedges and constructed labyrinths. In such a labyrinth at Woodstock was concealed the bower of "Fair Rosamund" ; and these grounds were more elaborately cultivated by Henry III. By this time, however, gardens had become much more general around the big houses, and fruits of many kinds were grown, including pears, apples, quinces, mulberries, medlars, cherries and peaches. King John is reported as having made himself seriously ill in an attempt to bury his chagrin in a surfeit of peaches and ale. By the middle of the fourteenth century, gardens were so common and so prolific that the gardeners employed by the Lords and citizens of London had set up a kind of market to sell their "pulse, cherries, vegetables and other wares to their trade pertaining" on a piece of ground "opposite to the church of St. Austin near the gate of St. Paul's Churchyard." This market, however, prospered and expanded to such an extent that it interfered with "persons passing both on foot and on horseback," and "the scurrility, clamour and nuisance of the gardeners and their servants" had become such an annoyance to the respectable neighbours and "such a nuisance to the priests who are singing matins and mass in the church of St. Austin, and to others, both clerks and laymen, in prayers and orisons there serving God," that a petition was addressed to the mayor and aldermen that the market might be removed to some more fitting place.

Some interesting details of one of these large London gardens are given in a roll preserved at the Record Office, giving an account of the possessions of Henry de Lacy, Earl of Lincoln, at the very end of the thirteenth century.

Whilst the gardens attached to great houses and castles were used as places of meeting and recreation, the garden of the ordinary farm or cottage was, in the fifteenth and earlier centuries, entirely utilitarian in aim—that is, it was a herb and vegetable garden. It was, indeed, regarded as an adjunct of the kitchen and the still-room ; and therefore was commonly part of the woman's province. Barnaby Googe, writing a hundred years later, said : "Herein were the olde husbandes very careful and used always to judge that where they found the Garden out of order, the wife of the house (for unto her belonged the charge thereof) was no good huswyfe."

The orchards and gardens of the monasteries and priories were also mainly occupied with fruit, vegetables, and savoury and medicinal herbs. William of Malmesbury, writing in the twelfth century, commented on the famous vineyards of Gloucestershire which, he said, "are more plentiful in crops and more pleasant in flavour than any in England." The survival in many towns of a "Vine Street" probably indicates both the existence and the site of twelfth and thirteenth century vineyards. The accounts of the Priory of Norwich, a number of which exist in manuscript, give details of the activities of the Monastery gardeners. The monastery

'LOVER ATTAINS THE ROSE'
Illumination from *Roman de la Rose*, Flemish MS. c. 1500

orchard contained mixed fruit trees, the apples and pears being used not
only for eating but for the making of cider and perry, large quantities of
these being made each year. In bad fruit years, the purchase of apples
and pears for the table is shown on the accounts ; but usually there seems
to have been an ample supply. This is likely enough, as many monasteries
had orchards of considerable extent, that at Llanthony Priory being
twelve acres in size. As early as 1175, a Papal Bull of Alexander III
confiscated the property of the monks of Winchenley in Gloucestershire,
this property including the town of Swiring, "with all its orchards."

By the end of the fourteenth century, the poorer parts of the com-
munity had established themselves in a better and more independent
position as against the autocracy of the lords of the soil. Instead of
rendering service to the landlord for so many days a week, they purchased
complete exemption by payment of rent, either in money or in kind, for
their little farms and holdings. Practically every cottage and farm thus

23

liberated had an orchard and garden round it. The very poor, indeed, lived almost entirely on vegetables. Langland, in *Piers Plowman*, says :

> "Al the povere peple tho
> Pescoddes fetten,
> Benes and baken apples
> Thei broghte in hir lappes,
> Chibolles and chervelles,
> And ripe chiries manye,"

and later, he says, the poorest folk,

> "With grene poret and pesen,
> To poisone hym [*Hunger*] thei thoghte."

Chaucer, too, in picturing the dire poverty of patient Griseldis, speaks of her dependence on vegetables, and of the fact that as she had no garden, she gathered the wayside herbs for her food :

> "Whan she homward cam she wolde bringe
> Wortes or othere herbes tyme ofte
> The which she shredde and seeth for her livinge."

Among the better-to-do, although vegetables still occupied a substantial space in the garden, more attention was paid to fruits and, later, to a considerable variety of flowers. Fruit was plentiful and cherries and strawberries were hawked in the town streets. Lydgate writes in *London Lackpenny*, of the cry of the street sellers :

> "Then unto London I dyd me hye,
> Of all the land it beareth the pryse
> 'Hot pescodes' one began to crye,
> 'Strabery rype' and 'cherryes in the ryse'."

In these larger gardens of the richer classes fruit was cultivated not only for its edible value but also for its beauty of flower and growth. Indeed, in an increasing number of these gardens restfulness, seclusion, and aesthetic qualities became the prime considerations. Paths were gravelled or sanded ; turf mounds, on which to sit and stand to look over the garden walls, were built up, and climbing and twining plants were so trained, often on trellises, as to produce arbours. The whole garden was surrounded by walls or thick hedges. Flowers were grown for their beauty and their scent, though the number of varieties was not great. We get good pictures of these late fourteenth century gardens from Chaucer's poems ; the arbour in *The Flower and the Leaf*

> "benched was, and eke with turfes newe,
> Freshly turved . . .
> And shapen was this herber, roofe and all,
> As is a pretty parlour ; and also
> The hegge as thicke as is a castle wall,
> So that who list withoute to stand or go,

By courtesy of the National Museum of Wales

HALSWELL HOUSE AND GROUNDS, SOMERSET

Oil painting by J. I. Richards, d. 1810

By courtesy of Mrs. Carline

A COTTAGE GARDEN AT STAPLEFORD, WILTSHIRE

Water colour by G. F. Carline, c. 1886

Though he would all day prien to and fro,
He shoulde not see if there were any wighte
Within or no ; but one within well mighte
Perceive alle that yeden there withoute."

The walled garden of Mirth, in the *Romaunt of the Rose*, gives a fair description of the garden of Chaucer's day, with its carpet of fresh flowers :

"There sprange the vyolet al newe,
And fresshe pervynke ryche of hewe,
And floures yelowe, white and rede;
Such plenty grewe there never in mede.
Ful gaye was al the grounde, and queynt,
And poudred, as men had it peynt,
With many a freshe and sondrye floure,
That casten up ful good savoure."

Roses were grown both for beauty and fragrance ; single and double, as well as the dog-rose and sweet-briar. The rose-bush in Mirth's garden drew the poet with its sweet scent.

During the middle years of the fifteenth century, interest in gardening on a luxurious scale reached a low ebb, owing to the new insecurity caused by the Wars of the Roses. The big houses took on the character of fortified castles, and, so far as might be, were built on the tops of hills. But, with the ending of these wars by the battle of Bosworth Field in 1485, and the accession of Henry VII to the throne, things became settled once more, and new houses of a different and more homely type were built in the valleys and on the lower slopes, where serious gardening was more possible. During the early years of the Tudor period, several novelties were introduced into these gardens, two of the most striking being the surrounding of flower-beds with low trellis-work, and the clipping of certain suitable trees and shrubs into quaint shapes—the art of topiary. Leland, writing in the early years of the sixteenth century, mentions two or three gardens in which examples of this art were to be found. At "Wresehill Castle" he describes an orchard with artificial mounts "opere topiario writhen about in degrees like turnings of cokilsheells to come to the top without payne," and refers to another garden, celebrated for its topiary, at Uskelle village, near Tewton. Reference has previously been made to the construction of mounts built against the walls of enclosed gardens, from the top of which views might be obtained of the surrounding country, and the approach of enemies might be observed. In Tudor times, these mounds or mounts became much more highly developed, becoming practically small artificial hills, built of earth, and planted with fruit trees, the winding paths leading up them bordered with flowers and herbs. At the top of many of these mounts was an arbour of varying degrees of permanence, some differing little from those of the previous century, some quite substantial little buildings of brick or stone. One of the most elaborate of these arbour-topped mounts was constructed in 1533 at the end of "The King's New Garden" at Hampton Court. The arbour, in this instance, was a very elaborate structure, largely of glass ; and payment was made for the lattice-work to "John, a gwylder smith," and to Galyon Hone, the King's glazier, for a number of items. Sometimes the more elaborate of these arbours were connected with others or with the house by galleries of poles and trellis, covered with vines and creepers, these galleries running along beside the garden walls.

Another innovation of the very earliest fifteenth century, distinct from the straight trellis-edged beds, were the "knotted" flower-beds, planned out to form interlacing geometrical patterns. Of the Hampton Court garden it was commented that it was so "enknotted it cannot be expressed." The ribbon-like strips of which these beds were composed were bordered with close clipped box plants or thrift or similar, low-growing tufted plants, or else by narrow edgings of brick or tile, flowers and small shrubs being planted between them, rather in the manner of Victorian carpet-bedding. Sometimes, instead of flowers, the strips were picked out with various coloured earths. Hampton Court gardens were also embellished with numerous brass sun-dials, and with carved animals holding vanes.

In the *Literary Magazine* in 1757 appeared, with copious extracts, a long review of Paul Hentzner's *Journey into England in the Year 1598*—that is, during the reign of Elizabeth—which was privately published at Strawberry Hill, only a few copies being printed for distribution among friends. Of the gardens at Nonsuch, another palace of Henry VIII, Hentzner gives us a clear picture. "Nonsuch, a royal retreat, in a place formerly called Cuddington, a very healthful situation, chosen by King Henry VIII for his pleasure and retirement, and built by him with an excess of magnificence and elegance, even to ostentation ; one would imagine everything that architecture can perform, to have been employed in this one work : there are everywhere so many statues, that seem to breathe, so many miracles of consummate art, so many charts that rival even the perfecting of Roman antiquity, that it may well claim and justify its name of Nonsuch, being without an equal, as the poet sung :

> This which no equal has in art or fame,
> Britons deservedly to Nonsuch name."

But gardens of this artificial and over-architectural kind were confined to the pleasure-grounds of a section of the nobility and the very rich. William Harrison, in his contribution to the second edition of Holinshed's Chronicles, in 1586-7, describes his own garden, and comments—possibly with some irony—on these knotted and statuary-loaded pleasaunces. "How art," he writes, "also helpeth nature, in the dailie colouring, dubling and inlarging the proportion of our floures, it is incredible tò report, for so curious and so cunning are our Gardeners now, in these daies, that they

TITLE PAGE

From *Paradisi In Sole Paradisus Terrestris* by John Parkinson, 1629

presume to doo in maner what they list with nature, and moderate hir course in things as if they were hir superiours. It is a world also to see how many strange hearbs, plants and annuall fruits, are dailie brought unto us from the Indies, Americans, Taprobane, Canarie Iles, and all parts of the world. . .''

A reaction from the extreme artificialities which had found their way into and, as most people nowadays would think, corrupted the reasonable formalism of the truly English garden, set in during the reign of Elizabeth. Significantly, this purge is evidenced in what is perhaps the finest essay on gardening ever written by an Englishman. In his celebrated *Essay on Gardens*, Bacon indicates the type of garden that appealed to a man of culture and taste in Elizabethan days. He has in mind the spacious garden of a man of wealth and position, for he describes the deliberate planning of a "princelike" garden covering not less than thirty acres of ground. This he would have "divided into three Parts : a Greene in the Entrance ; a Heath or Desart in the Going forth ; and the Maine Garden in the midst ; besides Alleys on both Sides. And I like well that Foure acres of Ground be assigned to the Green; six to the Heath ; Foure and Foure to either Side ; and Twelve to the Maine Garden. The Greene hath two pleasures ; the one, because nothing is more Pleasant to the Eye than Greene Grasse kept finely shorne; the other, because it will give you a faire Alley in the midst, by which you may go in front upon a Stately Hedge, which is to inclose the Garden. But, because the Alley will be long, and in great Heat of the Yeare, or Day, you ought not to buy the shade in the Garden by going in the Sunne thorow the Greene, therefore you are, of either Side the Greene, to Plant a Covert Alley, upon Carpenter's Worke, about Twelve Foot in Height, by which you may goe in

TULIP
Woodcut from Gerard's *Herball*

28

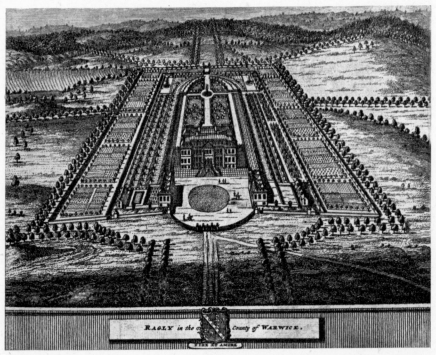

A FORMAL GARDEN
Seventeenth century engraving

Shade into the Garden. As for the Making of Knots or Figures, with Divers Coloured Earths, that they may lie under the Windowes of the House on that Side which the Garden stands, they be but Toyes: You may see as good Sights many times, in Tarts. The Garden is best to be Square, encompassed, on all the Foure Sides, with a stately Arched Hedge."

After giving a long list of flowers and shrubs "for the Climate of London," arranged to give beauty in the garden throughout the year— "that you may have *Ver Perpetuum*, as the Place Affords," Bacon goes on to enumerate those flowers and herbs which should be grown for their scent in the garden. "And because," he says, "the Breath of Flowers is farre Sweeter in the Aire (where it comes and Goes, like the warbling of Musick) than in the hand, therefore nothing is more fit for that Delight than to know what be the Flowers and Plants that doe best perfume the Aire. Roses Damask and Red are fast Flowers of their Smels ; so that you may walke by a whole Row of them, and finde Nothing of their Sweetnesse ; Yea, though it be in a Morning's Dew. Bayes likewise yeeld no Smell as they grow. Rosemary little, nor Sweet-Marjoram.

29

That which above all Others, yeelds the Sweetest Smell in the Aire, is the Violet ; specially the White-double-Violet, which comes twice a Yeare ; about the middle of Aprill, and about Bartholomew-tide. Next to that is the Muske-Rose. Then the Strawberry-Leaves dying, which yeeld a most Excellent Cordiall Smell. Then the Flower of the Vines : It is a little dust, like the dust of a Bent, which growes upon the Cluster in the first Comming forth. Then Sweet Briar. Then Wall-Flowers, which are very Delightfull to be set under a Parler or Lower Chamber Window. Then Pincks, and Gilly-Flowers, specially the Matted Pinck, and Clove Gilly-Flower. Then the Flowers of the Lime Tree. Then the Hony-Suckles, so they be somewhat afarre off. Of Beane Flowers I speake not, because they are Field Flowers. But those which Perfume the Aire most delightfully, not passed by as are the rest, but being Troden upon and Crushed, are Three : that is Burnet, Wilde-Thyme, and Water-Mints. Therefore you are to set whole Allies of them, to have the Pleasure, when you walke or tread." Even Bacon advised that the "Stately Arched Hedge," which encompassed the garden might well be surmounted, between the arches, by "little Figures, with Broad Plates of Round Coloured Glasse, gilt, for the Sunne to play upon." Yet it is on the beauty and fragrance of the plants and flowers that he chiefly dwells.

Arbours were still a common feature of Elizabethan gardens ; as were the mounts of earlier days. Some of these were arranged in the middle of the garden, and others were banked up against the outer walls. Of such, Bacon wrote : "At the end of both side grounds, I would have a mount of some pretty height, leaving the wall of the enclosure breast-high, to look abroad into the fields." In *Much Ado about Nothing*, Hero speaks of the arbour in Leonato's garden :

> "—— the pleached bower
> Where honey-suckles, ripen'd by the sun,
> Forbid the sun to enter."

It was in an arbour in his orchard that Mr. Justice Shallow gossiped with Falstaff, over a last year's pippin and a dish of caraways. Among the plants used for these pleached arbours were honey-suckle, jasmine, vines, roses, clematis or "Ladies' Bower"—"both white and red and purple, single and double."

Mazes, though examples of them had existed in England for a couple of centuries, became more popular as a feature of large gardens in the later years of Elizabeth's reign. William Lawson, in his *New Orchard and Garden*, issued in 1618, speaks of mazes, which, he says, "when they are well formed of a man's height, your friend may perhaps wander in gathering berries till he cannot recover himself without your help." Writing some half-century earlier, Thomas Hill gives two plans for such mazes ; commenting that though they are not "for any necessary commoditie

30

FLORA
Engraving from R. Blome's *The Gentleman's Recreation*, 1686

in a garden, those who so listeth may place the one of them in a void place that will best be spared for the only purpose to sport in them at times"; and he gives a list of some of the plants used in setting these mazes. The list includes "lavender, cotton spike, majoram, isope, time, quickset, privet, and plashed fruit trees."

"The art of Topiary" continued to be practised, though it devoted itself mainly—except in established topiary gardens—to the designing of rounded bushes, pyramids and other geometric forms. But here and there, more elaborate topiary work was carried out.

In later Tudor and early Stuart times, a very large number of new flowers from abroad—what Parkinson classed as "outlandish" flowers as distinct from "English" flowers—were introduced into the larger gardens of this country; especially the gardens of the more cultured among the well-to-do. These flowers were, for the most part, grown in beds—which were commonly spoken of as "open knots," in contradistinction to "closed knots" of previous times, which were more concerned with pattern than with interesting plants.

Parkinson names, among English flowers, many that had long been known in our gardens, such as violets, columbines, roses, primroses and marigolds; together with "flowers that being strangers unto us, and giving the beauty and bravery of their colours so early, before many of our own-bred flowers, the more to entice us to their delight." Of daffodils he says there are almost a hundred sorts "whereof many are so exceeding sweete that a very few are sufficient to perfume a whole chamber."

For standards in the hedges and borders he finds "the sort of roses" the fittest; with them the Cherry Bay, the Rose Bay or Oleander, and the white and purple syringa (lilac) are "all graceful and delightful to set at several distances in the borders of knots." Pyracantha or "Prickly Coral Tree" makes a fine evergreen hedge, "plashed or laid down." The Laurustinus "doth chiefly desire to be sheltered under a wall, where it will best thrive, and give you his beautiful flowers in Winter for your delight, in recompence of his fenced dwelling."

Flowers and scented leaves were much used to decorate and perfume houses, as well as for personal ornament. Gerard says that violets made into posies "are delightful to look on and pleasant to smell," and Parkinson says of the auriculas, that "their flowers, being many set together upon a stalke, doe seeme every one of them to bee a Nosegay alone of itselfe," and of wallflowers he writes that "the sweetnesse of the flowers causeth them to be generally used in Nosegayes, and to deck up houses"; for which latter also leaves and branches of box "serve both Summer and Winter." Scented flowers and herbs were also extensively used, together with coarser herbage, for the strawing or strewing of floors; and Parkinson mentions germander as being "much used as a strawing herbe for houses, being pretty and sweete."

32

By courtesy of the Artist and the Leicester Galleries, London

THE GREENHOUSE

Oil painting by Stanley Spencer, 1938

By courtesy of the Artist

A GARDEN AT HENDON

Water colour by H. D. Copsey

Even these few quotations from Parkinson's *Paradisi in Sole Paradisus terrestris* (literally translated, Park-in-sun's Earthly Paradise) will show the least sentimental reader how different a book is this Herbal from any other printed in England. Gerard's Herbal, for instance, the first edition of which was published in 1597, thirty years before the appearance of Parkinson's book, is, so far as enthusiasm and interest in the beauty of flowers and gardens are concerned, a mere dull summary of herbalist's "facts" ; and is, in large part, a direct translation of Dodoens' *History of Plants*—a herbal of great reputation on the Continent. Both Gerard and Parkinson were doctors, and both had great experience of the plants and flowers about which they wrote. Both had fine gardens in London, and both—especially Parkinson—were botanists of repute as well as gardeners.

In the course of the seventeenth century gardening ideas and practice —as might be expected with the coincident rapid changes in our political and social structure—experienced many transformations. During the eleven years of the Commonwealth, gardens, taking the colour of the time, became more utilitarian ; and existing gardens were largely broken up and made more fruitful and materially profitable. The Royal gardens at Nonsuch and Wimbledon were sold, and steps were taken to dispose even of Hampton Court. But Parliament decided to stay the order, with the result that it was still in public hands at Charles II's restoration.

Few new large gardens were laid out until after 1660. Still, the interlude was not without value, and interest. During those eleven years, appeared the first gardening book of John Evelyn, though the rest of his books were published after the Restoration. In the last forty years of the seventeenth century, appeared also Worlidge's *Systema Agriculturae* and *Systema Horticulturae*, as well as his excellent treatise on Cider, *Vinetum Britannicum*.

In these few decades were published also Sir William Temple's celebrated work, *Upon the Garden of Epicurus, or of Gardening in the year 1685*, and Ralph Austen's *A Treatise of Fruit Trees*, and his *Observations upon some part of Sir F. Bacon's Naturall History as it concerns fruit trees, fruits, and flowers*.

Evelyn's interesting *Kalendarium Hortense* went quickly through many editions, the first of which appeared in 1664. In this practical work Evelyn names the flowers to be planted and the garden work to be done in each month of the year ; dividing these plants according to their comparative tenderness into three classes, those "least patient of cold," those enduring second degree of cold and those "not perishing, but in excessive cold to be last set in or protected under matrasses or slighter coverings."

During this period, newly planned gardens, both actual and ideal, were, compared with such a one as Bacon's "princely garden," of much smaller size. John Rea's *Flora, Ceres, et Pomona*, which was published in 1676, suggested that "for a private gentleman 40 square yards fruit

A VIEW OF THE ROYAL PALACE AT HAMPTON COURT
Coloured engraving by Parr after Rigaud, 1751

and 20 flower is enough ; a wall all round of brick 9 feet high, and a 5 feet wall to divide the fruit and flower gardens."

In the second half of the seventeenth century, the tulip mania, in an attenuated form, spread from Holland and took possession of English gardeners. Even in the earlier part of the century, the tulip was greatly admired. Some established gardens included many beds devoted entirely to tulips, each bed being occupied by a different variety. But towards the end of the century the tulip beds became, even in modest gardens, the most highly prized feature. Parkinson, in his *Paradisus*, describes and illustrates several varieties, and an enormous number of variations from these.

In the latter part of the sixteenth century, bowling greens had become fashionable, and occupied space in most large gardens. Thomas Baskerville, speaking of Warwick Castle, said that within the gate, "is a fair Court, and within that, encompassed with a pale, a dainty bowling-green, set about with laurels, firs, and other curious trees." In the course of his *Journals*, he refers to public bowling greens in many small towns and attached to many of the inns at which he stayed.

It was in the earlier part of the seventeenth century, during the reign of Charles I, that the Earl of Danby founded and endowed at Oxford the first Botanical Garden in England. Put in charge of this garden was a Brunswicker, John Bobart. In 1648, he published a catalogue of the

34

plants in the garden, listing about sixteen hundred ; a thousand of which were species from overseas.

Towards the end of the seventeenth century appeared an essay in many ways comparable with Bacon's celebrated work. It was written by another man of letters, Sir William Temple, and published under the title : *Upon the Garden of Epicurus ; or of Gardening in the Year 1685*, It dealt with gardening in general, and especially with the famous garden at Moor Park in Hertfordshire, made by the Countess of Bedford, and familiar to Temple in his youth. In it Temple sets out his picture of the perfect garden, premising that : "In every garden Four Things are necessary to be provided for, Flowers, Fruit, Shade and Water, and whoever lays out a Garden without all these, must not pretend it in any Perfection. It ought to lie to the best Parts of the House, or to those of the Master's commonest Use, so as to be but like one of the Rooms out of which you step into another. . ."

At this time, there were still, as there had always been, many gardens, large and small, within London itself. After all, London was then in many ways comparable both in air and spaciousness with a large cathedral

A VIEW OF THE PHYSIC GARDENS IN THE UNIVERSITY OF OXFORD
Engraving by I. Green, 1773

35

city of to-day ; and the houses of nearly all citizens had attached to them serious gardens, some of considerable size. But even at the beginning of the century, Parkinson had begun to complain of the effect of the smoke of the "sea-coal," then coming into general use. In the very City itself, gardens of no mean proportions had been common. In his *Survey*, John Stow, who died in 1605 (having, by the way, been rewarded, in his 79th year, for a life devoted to public work, by a Licence to Beg, issued by James I), speaks of the house built in 1532 in Throgmorton Street by Thomas Cromwell. "This house being finished," he says, "and having some reasonable plot of ground left for a garden, he caused the pales of the gardens adjoining to the north part thereof on a sudden to be taken down ; twenty-two feet to be measured forth right into the north of every man's ground ; a line there to be drawn, a trench to be cast, a foundation laid, and a high brick wall to be built. My father had a garden there, and a house [summer-house] standing close to his south pale ; this house they loosed from the ground, and bare upon rollers into my father's garden twenty-two feet, ere my father heard thereof. No warning was given him, nor other answer, when he spake to the surveyors of that work, but that their master Sir Thomas commanded them so to do ; no man durst go to argue the matter, but each man lost his land, and my father paid his whole rent, which was 6s. 6d. the year, for that half which was left."

An interesting document which has been preserved is Gibson's *Short Account of Several Gardens Near London ; with Remarks on some Particulars wherein they Excel or are Deficient, Upon a View of them in December 1691*. In this manuscript, Gibson comments on twenty-eight more or less celebrated gardens, including a few market gardens, three of these latter being at Hoxton and one at Mile End. Of Clements, of Mile End, Gibson says that "He has vines in many places about old trees, which they wind about. He made wine this year of his white Muscadine, and white Frontinac, better I thought than any French white wine. He keeps a shop of seeds and plants in pots next the street."

Evelyn's garden at Deptford and Raynton's garden at Enfield are briefly described without enthusiasm ; but, of all the gardens he deals with, evidently that of Dr. Uvedale, also at Enfield, was the one he most admired. He speaks of Uvedale as "a great lover of plants, and, having an extraordinary art in managing them, is become master of the greatest and choicest collection of exotic greens that is perhaps anywhere in this land. But, to speak of the garden in the whole, it does not lie fine to please the eye, his delight and care lying more in the ordering particular plants than in the pleasing view and form of his garden." Dr. Uvedale evidently had the same attitude towards plants and gardens as that of Canon Ellacombe, Forbes-Watson, and, indeed, of many of us to-day.

Just before the end of the seventeenth century, several translations of French gardening works were published in England ; John Evelyn and

ESHER IN SURREY, THE SEAT OF THE RT. HON. HENRY PELHAM, AS LAID OUT BY MR. KENT, 1798
Coloured engraving after W. Woollet from *Observations on Modern Gardening*

London and Wise (both, at that time, partners in the Brompton Nurseries)
being among the most celebrated of the translators. These two gardeners
were also fashionable garden designers. The garden of Sir Richard Child,
at Wanstead, was designed by London, and described in 1714 by Daniel
Defoe, in his *Journey Through England and Scotland*. He speaks of "the
noble seat of Sir Richard Child, with the finest garden in the world.
You descend from the salon into the parterre, which hath a canal in the
middle ; on the right a wilderness, and on the left a fine green walk,
which ends in a banqueting house. On one side of this green walk stands
the green-house, finely adorned with statues, and uncommonly furnished
with greens ; while behind this green-house are variety of high-hedged
walks affording delicious vistas. At the bottom of the canal is a bowling-
green encircled with grottos and seats, with antique statues between each
seat ; this bowling-green is separated by a balustrade of iron from another
long green walk, which leads you to another long canal."

In 1670 appeared the first edition of what proved to be a popular work :
The English Gardener, by Leonard Meager, who, for many years, was a
gardener at Warkworth, in Northamptonshire. He favoured quiet,
"neatly-ordered" gardens, of a kind which people were beginning to regard
as old-fashioned. In 1697, he wrote another book called *The New Art
of Gardening ; With the Gardener's Almanack*, spoken of by G. W. Johnson

in his *History of English Gardening,* as one of the classics of gardening ; in a modest way reminiscent of Parkinson and Bacon.

A pupil of London and Wise was Stephen Switzer, whose *The Nobleman's, Gentleman's and Gardener's Recreation* was published in 1715—appearing again with added matter in 1718 under the title *Ichnographia Rustica,* "by which title is meant the general Designing and Distributing of County Seats into gardens, woods, Parks, Paddocks, &c. : which I therefore call forests, or in more easie stile, Rural gardening."

In this book, Switzer expresses his admiration of and allegiance to Pope ; and, as the extracts quoted show, advocates that "rural" style which gradually took the place of the older *Grand Manier* of Le Nôtre and his school. The reference to Pope brings us to the beginning of a period of quite understandable reaction from the extreme and in many ways absurd formalism which, at the opening of the eighteenth century, marked an increasing number of gardens of almost every size. The war between formal and so-called Landscape gardening was beginning. The new school was backed by energetic propagandists among accepted men of letters. In 1712, Joseph Addison wrote in the *Spectator* that "our British gardeners, instead of humouring Nature, love to deviate from it as much as possible. Our trees rise in Cones, Globes and Pyramids. We see the marks of the scissars upon every Plant and Bush. I do not know whether I am singular in my opinion, but, for my own part, I would rather look upon a tree in all its Luxuriancy and Diffusion of Boughs and Branches, than when it is thus cut and trimmed into a Mathematical Figure ; and cannot but fancy that an Orchard in Flower looks infinitely more delightful than all the little Labyrinths of the most finished Parterre."

GARDEN PERSPECTIVE
Engraving from Repton's *Observations on the Theory & Practice of Landscape Gardening,* 1803

38

FORCING GARDENS IN WINTER
Aquatint from Repton's *Fragments on the Theory & Practice of Landscape Gardening*, 1816

In the following year, Pope, in an article in the *Guardian*, made a semi-humorous attack on the inartistic extravagancies of the fashionable gardens and gardeners of the time.

So early in the century as 1728, Batty Langley, in his *New Principles of Gardening*, wrote, "Is there anything more shocking than a stiff, regular garden?" When Sir Richard Temple died, at the very end of the seventeenth century, Lord Cobham, Temple's son, began the gardens at Stow. These grew at a tremendous pace, covering, by 1755, a space of five hundred acres. The first designer was Bridgman, subsequently made chief gardener to the King, who laid out the grounds and planned the whole garden. Lord Percival, who visited the gardens in 1724, in a letter to his brother said that "the gardens, by reason of the good contrivance of the walks, seem to be three times as large as they are." Later, he said : "What adds to the bewty of this garden is that it is not bounded by a wall, but by a Ha-ha, which leaves you the sight of a bewtifull woody country, and makes you ignorant how far the high planted walks extend." Horace Walpole, in his essay on *Modern Gardening*, published in 1785, gives an interesting summary of the early history of the new movement. After referring to Temple's description of Moor Park in Hertfordshire, in Lady Bedford's time, mentioned earlier in this book, Walpole goes on to say : "But as no succeeding generation in an opulent and luxurious country

39

contents itself with the perfection established by its ancestors, more perfect perfection was still sought ; and improvements had gone on, till London and Wise had stocked our gardens with giants, animals, monsters, coats-of-arms and mottoes in yew, box and holly. Absurdities could go no farther, and the tide turned. Bridgman, the next fashionable designer of gardens, was far more chaste ; and whether from good sense, or that the nation had been struck and reformed by the admirable paper in the *Guardian*, No. 173, he banished the verdant sculpture, and did not even revert to the square precision of the foregoing age.''

Walpole says of Bridgman : ''I have observed in the garden at Gubbins, in Hertfordshire, many detached thoughts, that strongly indicate the dawn of modern taste. . . But the capital stroke, the leading step to all that has followed, was (I believe the first thought was Bridgman's) the destruction of walls for boundaries, and the invention of fosses—an attempt then deemed so astonishing that the common people called them Ha ! Ha ! to express their surprise at finding a sudden and unperceived check to their walks.''

Bridgman was followed by Kent, a famous name in the annals of horticulture. Walpole characterises him as ''painter enough to taste the charms of landscape, bold and opinionative enough to dare and to dictate, and born with a genius to strike out a great system from the twilight of imperfect essays. He leaped the fence,'' says our author, ''and saw that all nature was a garden.'' One of Kent's principles was that ''Nature abhors a straight line'' ; therefore all straight walks and straight hedges were anathema to his new school of landscape gardeners.

Perhaps the name with which people are most familiar as a pioneer and exponent of landscape gardening is that of Lancelot Brown. He was born in 1715, and brought up as a kitchen-gardener at Stow. He remained with Lord Cobham until 1750, when he was appointed Royal Gardener at Hampton Court. He became the fashionable garden designer, and was given the job of re-designing nearly all the great gardens in the country ; gaining the nickname of ''Capability'' Brown, from his habit of saying of nearly every garden he was asked to re-form, that it ''had great capabilities.'' He swept away the ages-old beauties of dozens of the loveliest of English gardens. Brown had an incredible influence on the majority of owners of big gardens, hardly a dozen of which he allowed to retain the features of which their owners had previously been so proud. He refused work in Ireland, because he said that he ''had not yet finished England.'' Tunnard, in his *Gardens in the Modern Landscape*, published in 1938, says that ''the demand for Brown's services was enormous, not because he did good work, but because improvements were the fashion. His genial manner won him popularity, and the literary and grammatical allusions with which he invariably illustrated his ideas no doubt helped to produce, in a gullible public, the sense of a competence which he was,

By courtesy of the Artist

THE BACKYARD, LANSCOMBE FARM, COCKINGTON, DEVONSHIRE
Oil painting by Dorothy Belasco

VIEW FROM THE GARDEN AT LADYWOOD, GRASMERE, WESTMORLAND
Oil painting by Gilbert Spencer, 1942
By courtesy of the Artist and the Leicester Galleries, London

in fact, far from possessing." In time, small villa gardeners did their best to be in the prevailing fashion.

Cowper, in his poem, *The Garden*, gives expression to what later became a general sentiment:

> "Improvement too, the idol of the age,
> Is fed with many a victim. Lo, he comes!
> The omnipotent magician, Brown, appears!
> Down falls the venerable pile, the abode
> Of our forefathers . . .
> He speaks—the lake in front becomes a lawn;
> Woods vanish, hills subside, and valleys rise."

Cowper himself evidently had no use for the new theoretical garden designers. He said: "I write in a nook that I call my boudoir; it is a summerhouse no bigger than a sedan-chair; the door of it opens into the garden that is now crowded with pinks, roses and honeysuckles, and the window into my neighbour's orchard.

"I sit with all the windows and the door wide open, and am regaled with the scent of every flower, in a garden as full of flowers as I have known how to make it."

Overwhelming as had been the effect of Brown's and Bridgman's propaganda on the owners of stately gardens, and on the fashion-following villa gardeners, the great majority of English gardens and gardeners were far from converted, as the quotation from Cowper illustrates. Many even of those who favoured what they called landscape gardening interpreted the term in a very different way from that of the wholesale iconoclasts. Towards the end of the eighteenth century, Sir William Chambers, himself a professed disciple of the "landscape school," said: "Our virtuosi have scarcely left an acre of shade, or three trees growing in a line, from the Land's End to the Tweed."

"Capability" Brown died in 1784; by which time serious doubts as to the wisdom of much of his teaching were increasing amongst his erstwhile admirers. In that or the following year, Humphry Repton, describing himself as a professional landscape gardener, rapidly attracted an extensive clientele. In 1795, he published *Sketches and Hints on Landscape Gardening*. Especially at first, he defended much of Brown's theory, but seriously differed from much of it. The outstanding characteristic of Brown's landscapes was their smooth and bald surface: "Why," Repton asked, "this art has been called 'landscape gardening,' perhaps he who gave it the title may explain. I can see no reason, unless it be the efficacy which it has shown in destroying landscapes, in which, indeed, it seems infallible."

"The house," he writes, "the buildings, the gardens, the roads, the bridges, and every circumstance which marks the habitation of man must be artificial; and although in the works of art we may imitate the forms and graces of Nature, yet to make them truly natural, always leads to absurdity." Repton goes on to expound his interpretation of the term "landscape gardening." He writes : "To improve the scenery of a country, and to display its native beauties with advantage, is an Art which originated in England, and has therefore been called *English Gardening ;* yet as this expression is not sufficiently appropriate, especially since gardening, in its more confined sense of *Horticulture,* has been likewise brought to its greatest perfection in this country, I have adopted the term *Landscape Gardening,* as most proper, because the art can only be advanced and perfected by the united powers of the *landscape painter* and the *practical gardener.*" He defines his principles thus :

"The perfection of Landscape Gardening consists in the four following requisites : First, it must display the natural beauties, and hide the natural defects of every situation. Secondly, it should give the appearance of extent and freedom, by carefully disguising or hiding the boundary. Thirdly, it must studiously conceal every interference of art, however expensive, by which the Scenery is improved ; making the whole appear the production of Nature only ; and fourthly, all objects of mere convenience or comfort, if incapable of being made ornamental, or of becoming parts of the natural scenery, must be removed or concealed."

The beginning of the nineteenth century almost exactly coincided with the beginning of a reaction from the absolutism of the false landscape school of Brown and his colleagues. The quotations from Repton's writings, at the end of the eighteenth century, show the form that this reaction was taking ; and, with occasional lapses into conservatism, the trend moved steadily towards the characteristic English garden of the Elizabethan age. In 1839, we find the Rev. Thomas James writing : "Landscape gardening has encroached too much upon gardening proper ; and this has had the same effect upon our gardens that horticultural societies have had on our fruits—to make us entertain the vulgar notion that size is virtue. If I am to have a system at all, give me the good old system of terraces and angled walks, and clipt yew hedges, against whose dark and rich verdure the bright old-fashioned flowers glittered in the sun."

Three years later, the same writer, in a couple of articles in the *Quarterly Review* and *The Carthusian,* described a plan intended to "combine the chief excellencies of the artificial and natural styles ; keeping the decorations immediately about the house formal, and so passing on by gradual transition to the wildest scenes of nature." James showed himself a true descendant of Bacon and other garden-lovers of the Elizabethan age in his appreciation of the peaceful beauty of native English landscape, and of the charm and fragrance of English flowers.

A few years later, in 1850, J. C. Loudon, a popular writer on practical gardening subjects, died ; but, in the same year, his widow—herself a keen gardener—published a work of his called *The Villa Gardener.* This

'VIEW FROM THE RUSTIC SEAT, SHRUBLANDS'
19th century coloured lithograph by E. A. Brooke from *Gardens of England*

was described on the title-page as dealing with "The laying-out, planting and culture of garden and grounds, in extent from one perch to fifty acres and upwards." This book shows the sensible compromise which had, by informed persons with taste and judgment, been arrived at between the two extremist points of view. "Whatever style," Loudon writes, "may be adopted by the architect and landscape gardener both artists must be guided . . . by certain rules, deduced from fundamental principles. Whatever, either in a building or a garden, cannot be justified on fundamental principles, must undoubtedly be wrong ; and whatever cannot be referred to pre-established rules must necessarily be new, and may be either right or wrong, according to its consistency or inconsistency with fundamental principles. . . When any part is produced, either of a building or a garden, for which no sufficient reason can be given, that part must be either a superfluity or a deformity.

"*The fitness of the means employed to the end to be obtained* is the most important principle, applicable both to architecture and gardening as useful arts.

"*In Gardening* the principles of fitness, or the adjustment of the means to the end, may be applied to the situation of the garden ; to the fitness

43

of the soil for the articles to be cultivated ; to the fitness of the forms of the compartments for carrying on the processes of cultivation ; to the fitness of the culture for the particular plants cultivated, and so on."

Elsewhere, he says : "The principle of the recognition of art . . . is recognisable in every description of human improvement. . . We have considered it necessary to insist on this principle here, in order that our readers may go along with us when we come to make the application of it to the modern style of landscape gardening. This style is said to be an imitation of nature ; and in consequence, many persons have argued in favour of imitating nature so closely as to produce scenes which might be mistaken for natural ones. . . If we are right in our principle, however, such facsimile imitations of nature, even of the most beautiful nature that can be selected, constitute but a very inferior style of art ; and the landscape gardener who should produce a piece of water surrounded by grass and trees . . . in such a natural-looking manner that it might be selected for copying from by a landscape painter and mistaken by him for a piece of natural scenery, has exactly the same pretension to the character of an artist as a manufacturer of artificial flowers or wax figures."

In the same year appeared the first edition of another popular handbook, titled *How To Lay Out a Garden*, by Edward Kemp, Landscape Gardener. This book, like Loudon's, shows the interpretation now being given to the term "landscape gardening" by practical men, and accepted by an increasing section of the public. Here are one or two significant extracts.

"Few characteristics of a garden contribute more to render it agreeable than *snugness* and *seclusion*. They serve to make it appear peculiarly one's own, converting it into a kind of *sanctum*. A place that has neither of these qualities might almost as well be public property. Those who love their garden often want to walk, work, ruminate, read, romp, or examine the various changes and developments of Nature in it ; and to do so unobserved. All that attaches us to a garden and renders it a delightful and cherished object, seems dashed and marred if it has no privacy."

"Art should be pretty obviously expressed in that part of every garden which is in the immediate vicinity of the house, and may sometimes retain its prominence throughout the whole place. In the latter case, terraces, straight lines of walks, avenues of trees or shrubs, rows of flower-beds, and geometrical figures, with all kinds of architectural ornaments, will prevail. Considerable dignity of character may certainly thus be acquired ; and, if well sustained, the expression of high art will be a very noble one. But there are not many places which will bear to be thus treated, and it is less frequently suitable for one of small dimensions."

During the previous century or more, whilst these freakish changes in garden fashion were taking place, there had been a continuously increasing introduction into England of foreign flowering plants, trees and

THE KITCHEN GARDEN IN OCTOBER
Oil painting by Harry Bush

shrubs. On the practice of real gardeners, indifferent to the vagaries of fashion, these new flowering plants were having a great effect. Well before the middle of the nineteenth century, the more brilliantly decorative of these importations were in something like general cultivation. Handbooks on the cultivation of these flowers began to appear and met with considerable public demand. Thus, in the second decade of the century,

45

was published, *A Practical Treatise on the Growth and Culture of the Carnation, Pink, Auricula, Polyanthus, Ranunculus, Tulip, Hyacinth, Rose and other Flowers, By Thomas Hogg, Florist, Paddington Green*, a second edition being called for in 1822. It describes in much detail the various expert methods of cultivation of these so-called "florist's flowers," the number of named varieties of each being fabulous. Thus, over a hundred varieties of carnation are listed. A few years later, in 1836, Thomas Willats brought out *The Florist Cultivator : with select lists of the finest Roses, Geraniums, Carnations, Pinks, Auriculas, Tulips, Dahlias, Heartsease, &c.* In this book, six hundred and sixty-three species of flowers and shrubs are briefly described, with directions for their cultivation.

Many owners of gardens, particularly of gardens of modest size, were concerned only with the cultivation of these relatively new flowers under conditions which best promoted the production of plants with fine showy blooms, regardless of the form and structure of the garden as a whole. They were plant and flower lovers, rather than garden lovers. Before the final quarter of the century was reached, this interest in individual plants and their cultivation had spread widely, not only among the devotees of specimen flowers and florist's varieties but also among those with more catholic tastes, whose main interest was in the healthy growth of individual plants, yet who also recognised as important the part which should be played by the garden's form and structure—at any rate near the house.

The interest taken in individual plants, especially those hardy in this climate, each allowed scope for natural growth, though grouped harmoniously and with an eye to broad effect, allowance being made for some degree of formality near the house, grew steadily as the century moved towards its close. The way was prepared by Forbes-Watson's charming *Flowers and Gardens*, published in 1872, by Henry Bright's *English Flower-garden* and *A Year in a Lancashire Garden*, and several books by keen amateurs like Canon Ellacombe. But the writer who had far and away the greatest influence on the garden-loving public was William Robinson (referred to in the Introduction), the editor and founder of several important gardening journals, and the author of book after book on the practical cultivation and arrangement of hardy plants and shrubs. To him we chiefly owe the herbaceous border and the modern rock garden—a very different thing from the "rockeries" of the big gardens of the Middle Ages. Robinson's point of view broadened a little as time went on, until it differed little from that of William Morris, who wrote, in *Hopes and Fears for Art*, "Large or small, the garden should look both orderly and rich. It should be well fenced from the outer world. It should by no means imitate either the wilfulness or the wildness of Nature, but should look like a thing never seen except near a house." There was, indeed, a tendency on the part of many of the new garden

'Helping the War Effort': London Gardens in Wartime
Oil painting by Helen Copsey

enthusiasts to oust all formality from their gardens, even though those gardens were five or more acres in area. What had, throughout the generations, been the appropriate—indeed natural and necessary—informality of the English cottage garden, was not necessarily appropriate to these gardens of larger size. Of those of the newer school, who cared for individual plants and their free growth, were some who recognised that the unexaggerated formalism of the Elizabethan gardens was not quite irrelevant. Thus, Henry Bright, writing in 1881, said that "The English Flower garden may afford far greater pleasure than it does at present. We must learn to look on plants, not as mere points of colour, but as old friends on whose coming we can rely, and who, returning with the recurring seasons, bring back with them pleasant memories of past years."

Writing about ten years earlier, Forbes-Watson says: "We find flower-beds habitually considered too much as masses of colour, instead of an assemblage of living beings. . . Gardeners are teaching us to think too little about the plants individually, and to look at them chiefly as an

47

assemblage of beautiful colours. It is difficult in these blooming masses to separate one from another, all produce so much the same sort of impression. The consequence is that people see the flowers in the beds without caring to know anything about them, or even to ask their names." The chief distinctive mark of the new movement was the appreciation of the beauty of individual plants ; in contrast not only with the purely architectural conception of a garden, but also with the carpet-bedding and "bedding-out" practices which characterised the Victorian age.

Two years after the publication of Bright's little book, William Robinson brought out the first edition of what has become the greatest and most popular contemporary garden classic, *The English Flower Garden*.

The future history of the English garden is doubtful. Everything depends on whether the common man becomes vocal and assertive, or whether with his traditional modesty he leaves everything to be decided by "leaders" who claim to know what is best for him. The findings of the recent Mass-observation enquiry on Housing into the real desires and aspirations of various groups of working people, establish the fact that although a number of the "observed" were unaccustomed to visualise a world in which they had any right of choice, over eighty per cent of the total pictured their ideal home as a small convenient house "with a garden." Should this bit of democracy materialise, the English cottage garden will have come into its own :

> "Where the marjoram once, and sage and rue,
> And balm and mint, with curled-leaf parsley grew,
> And double marigolds, and silver thyme,
> And pumpkins 'neath the window used to climb ;
> And where I often, when a child, for hours
> Tried through the pales to get the tempting flowers ;
> As lady's-laces, everlasting peas,
> True-love-lies-bleeding, with the hearts at ease,
> And golden-rods, and tansy running high,
> That o'er the pale-top smiled on passer-by."